Kahlo

The World Split Open

Kahlo:
The World Split Open

by

Linda Frank

BuschekBooks

Ottawa

Library and Archives Canada Cataloguing in Publication

Frank, Linda, 1951-
    Kahlo : the world split open / by Linda Frank.

Poems.
Includes text in Spanish.
ISBN 978-1-894543-48-4

    1. Kahlo, Frida--Poetry. I. Title.

PS8561.R2777K34 2008   C811'.6   C2008-904307-3

Cover Image: based on the photograph "Frida Kahlo|Graffiti in
the United States|Los Angeles, California", Wikimedia Commons,
downloaded June 15, 2008. Permission for use granted by Patrice
Raunet.

Printed by Hignell Book Printing, Winnipeg, Manitoba, Canada.

BuschekBooks
P.O. Box 74053, 5 Beechwood Avenue
Ottawa, Ontario, K1M 2H9 Canada

BuschekBooks gratefully acknowledges the support of the Canada
Council for the Arts for its publishing program.

**Canada Council
for the Arts**   **Conseil des Arts
du Canada**

For Allison and Caitlin

Table of Contents

iii. My Body is Plunged in Oranges

iv. I Am a Storm-Beaten Window

Acknowledgements

Thanks to John Buschek of BuschekBooks.

Thanks to the journals where some of these poems first appeared, many in earlier versions: *The Antigonish Review, CV2, Canadian Womens' Studies, The Dalhousie Review, Hammered Out, Other Voices, Poetry Canada* and *The Windsor Review.*

Thanks to the members of the Hamilton Poetry Centre workshop for their input on the poems and a special thanks to members of the Little Workshop, Jeffery Donaldson, Marilyn Gear Pilling, Bernadette Rule and John Terpstra who encouraged the poems into a full manuscript right from the beginning.

I owe a great debt of gratitude to the members of my writing workshop, Ross Belot, Dick Capling and Marilyn Gear Pilling for all their hard work and generosity every week on these poems and for the great time I had with them and Frida in Tobermory and Southampton.

A special thanks to Ross for editing beyond the call of duty and flying with me (not an enviable task for anyone) to Saltspring Island. Thanks to Robert Hilles for his generous reading, editing and encouragement on Saltspring. A special thank you to Bill and Simin for their hospitality in Vancouver, for inviting me to stay and work on the final edits in their dining room overlooking English Bay where eagles are a dime a dozen.

Thank you Marilyn for everything.

And as always, thank you Ken for your love and unconditional support.

Balconies Must Open

Balconies Must Open

Corsets. How many corsets
Leather, steel, plaster. I paint them
gentian blue, iodine red, all the colours
I want to adorn my corsets
Make them obscene

They hung me by my head from a beam
for hours to dry my cast. They put me
into traction, pulled my spine with weights

Painting is my own true medicine
My paintings, the babies I will never have

Under my high brow, crowned
with braids, hides death
I must paint
everything. My lips
my blood-red fingernails, eyelids
earlobes, eyelashes, eyebrows
I draw my dreams, my birth, my nudity
my blood, my blood, my blood

I paint myself until two of me exist
I cast out the wounded Frida
The Frida inside is the one
on the canvas
She is me

Only I can tolerate her
She weeps, she has fever, she's in heat
She's ferocious. She lusts
for a man, for a woman
A desire that exhausts
and empties her

My body is a Judas
but my hands don't fail me
They write a diary, send love-notes
scribble grocery lists, pick up scissors
cut my hair, dress me
like a man, button my fly

The hands you see are the same hands
that embrace Diego
pinch the nipple of a desired woman
hold the brush

Above all, they hold the brush

I draw each little hair of my monkeys
each little hair of my moustache. Every
gland in my nurse's breast, heavy
with milk

I want to be loved by the brilliant blue sky
the watermelons in the market, the wistful eyes
of animals. I want to be loved by millions
I want the world to fall
head over heels in love with Frida

I believe in love. I believe
that balconies must open
and women must fly out
I fly after Diego

I am afraid to lose those I love
I want everyone
to turn and look
to look at me

How It Started

All that time alone, lying
on my back under a mirror
canopy. I was all I had
to look at. And so it started

I painted what I saw
Nothing more
I painted myself
I was the subject
I knew best

Later, when I saw
the photograph my father
had taken of me after
the accident, I wanted to refuse
the suffering I saw
in my eyes. From then on
for every photo I stared
directly into the lens, straight out
from every canvas

Look at what surrounds me
Look at my hair, my dress
my jewelry, the parrots
and monkeys and the dogs. See
how they push the pain
off the canvas

The Prepatoria

Fifteen and thrust into the heart
of Mexico City just as her country
is bursting into life, reinventing itself
and she's in the middle of it all
The street vendors and public gardens
movie houses, everyone in debate
declaring their allegiance
to the left or the right, her country
embroiled in cultural and political
ferment with the birth of *mesitaje*
its message sprawled in revolutionary
murals across the walls of the Prepatoria

And she has disdain for the girls
she thinks trite, spoiled, *cursi*
irritated by their gossip. She dresses
in blue overalls, cycles with the boys
Carries her knapsack filled with texts
notebooks, drawings, butterflies
dried flowers. And she reads
She reads everything

And falls in love
With socialism and with Alejandro
leader of the *Cachuchas*, and yes
he's her boyfriend, and she calls him
her *novio*, but he thinks a fiancé is bourgeois
and will merely call himself her intimate
friend. He is dedicated only
to Mexico's great destiny

The First Self Portrait

was for Alejandro. A dark
melancholy offering
to a boy she knew she was losing
Hang it in a low place, she told him
Where you can see it as if
you were looking at me

She painted her hand extended, asking
for someone to hold it. Her face is cool
and reserved. For the first and last time
the eyes hold a hint of fragility

She painted a plunging neckline, the flesh
of her breasts pale, her nipples
prominent through the velvet
A wine-red dress, the folds
soft, the collar and cuffs a gold brocade
A slender and elongated Modigliani
alone against a dark ocean and sky

After Alex leaves, she takes a sharp-edged knife
and with a frozen smile scrapes the paint
from the canvas so slowly that the sound
of the steel against the dry oil paint
is a raw rasp moan

From then on she always paints
the same expression, her eyes
a mask of dignity and determination
But she paints her body naked
Her body bears her agony on the canvas
Reveals the cost of creating
each new self

Arabesque

Yesterday I was a girl
walking on the street with a boy
who bought me a toy parasol. I lost it
and we searched for it and missed
our bus, and I was so sad not to have it
He bought me a new cup and ball instead
Yesterday I was a girl
who climbed onto the next bus
with the boy of my dreams, a bus
that was crushed by a streetcar
and shattered into pieces

And then I was a girl lying naked
on that street, impaled on the metal
handrail the way a bull is skewered
by a sword. I thought only to find
my pretty coloured cup and ball.
I had no tears. My blood was sprinkled
with powdered gold spilled
from a house painter's bag, and I heard
people call for help for the little ballerina
Because of the gold glistening with my blood
they thought I was a gilded dancer

Yesterday I was a girl
innocent and whole. And then
I was broken and bloody and carried
to a nearby pool hall by a man
in overalls who placed his knee on my chest
and pulled out the steel rod
that had penetrated my hip and exited
through my vagina. I heard the sound
of my own bones breaking

The boy covered me with his coat. I screamed
louder than the sirens of the ambulance

Yesterday my life was opaque
with mystery. In seconds
I learned everything

Accident Report

Dislocation of left shoulder

Dislocation of left elbow

Eleven fractures of the right leg

Right foot dislocated and crushed

Fracture of the third and fourth ribs

Broken clavicle

Pelvis fractured
in three places

Fracture
of the cervical vertebrae

Spinal column broken
in three places
in lumbar region

Acute peritonitis

Abdominal wound produced
by metal rod entering
at the hip and exiting
through the genitals

> *Every time they move me*
> *I cry a litter of tears*

Wings of a Grounded Angel

They Ask For Planes and Are Given Straw Wings, painted in
1938

The hunter will jess a falcon
tether it with leather to keep it
bound. I paint the wings
of a grounded angel, straw wings
of loneliness suspended by ribbons
that fall from the sky and encircle my
body. Ribbons nailed by their bows to the ground

I fly, holding the hand
of my double, the girl who understands
the girl who can dance and laugh and move
so freely. The girl who pulls me to the world
of flight through the hot breath door I draw
with my index finger on the steamy glass
of my bedroom window

The Broken Column
Painted in 1944

This is how she paints it
Her fractured body
stark against an immense
and barren plain. A cloudless sky
blue grey and ominous, low
over ravines cut deep
into the arid earth. Her body
and the sterile land
beyond touch

Her torso split open
like a tropical fruit
Her spine a crumbling ruin
Her broken body held together
by a prison of leather straps
and metal buckles. The passion
and pain revealed in perfect breasts, life
on a body cruelly cleaved
from loin to neck. Dozens of tiny nails
pierce the naked skin, pierce
even those beautiful naked breasts

I Paint My Own Reality

because my body is the canvas
of my self and to paint myself
over and over is how
I claim it from the margins

because my broken body
is politic, history, country
love, pain, the whole world

because anything that escapes
the canvas escapes the body
but paint remembers, pushes through
pentimento

because I want to split the world
wide open

A Parrot Screaming

The Delicate Dove Charms The Fat Frog

He ate and slept up on his scaffold, painted
his own vocabulary of colour. People came
to watch. He was the magnet and they iron filings
He, the fat frog high on his lily-pad platform
painted non-stop, an addict to the paint
to the performance. He told tales of eating
human flesh, young female flesh, he said
wrapped in tortillas like the tenderest pig

Oh she knew who he was
this mythic muse of the revolution

His Mestizos and Amerindians toiled
in the fields and mines all over the walls
of the city. His workers' collectives
sprawled the Mexican landscape
He painted the folklore and the folk
And of course the women. She knew
that to model for him was to offer your body
to his flesh as well as to his eyes

She was seventeen, he forty-one
when she stood below his scaffold. Her long
dark hair blanketed thin, delicate shoulders
Thick eyebrows met above her nose
like the wings of a blackbird silhouetted
on the milky sky of her flawless skin
Come down, she called to him. *Come down and look
at my paintings. I brought you portraits of women
and one of them is me*

And when a few days later he kissed her for the first time
her father told him, *She is a devil*
and handed him a photograph taken of her
standing in a doorway, one dove cupped
in the palm of her right hand, one dove
perched on the fingers of her left, ready to fly

Somewhere Lovers Were Dancing

Diego, Lupe and Frida all sat in her father's garden
on a Sunday afternoon. Hibiscus
bougainvillea and coralbells red hot
between the tamarind trees. Nightingales
murmured in their bamboo cages, swung sleepy
from the limbs of the orange and cashew trees
Seeds of the habilla exploded in the heat
Green grapefruit hung from the branches, clung
to the trunks of the cirian, pregnant
with the moment, ripe and ready to burst

When Diego and Lupe got home, Lupe beat
at her husband's bulk with her fists, smashed
his collection of pre-Columbian carvings
and served the shards to him in a bean soup

On the night he took Frida from her father's house
the evening was hot, the air thick and tropical
fireflies sparked in the humid summer sky
They strolled the cactus and yucca-lined
streets of Coyoacán. The air was fragrant
with cocoanut, mango and papaya. Scent
of vanilla cut sharp by the sting of eucalyptus

Somewhere, lovers were dancing wild
to the cacophony of mariachi bands
They paused under a street lamp. When
their lips touched, the street lights went dark
When they parted, the lamps ignited
Lightning forked splinters across the Mexican sky

The Wedding

She knew even then. Even as she arranged
for the ceremony in the ancient city hall
in Coyacoán, even as she stood beside him
for the rites by the town mayor
who was also the local *pulqué* dealer
She knew the man she married
could never be anyone's husband
how spectacular his infidelity would become

There are many stories about where the wedding
party was held. In the house of Roberto Monenegro
On the roof of Tina Modotti's home
guests dancing between pieces
of Tina's lingerie hung out on lines to dry

Did Diego know? Even as he drank
too much tequila, waved his pistol
over his head, shot at a phonograph
broke a man's finger and sent Frida home crying
to her parents' house so they spent their wedding night
apart. Did he know how jealous of her love
he would become?

Sacred Monsters

Diego painted from early morning
until he lost the light and was still ready
for the nighttime, me beside him
glass for glass. As the bottle emptied
he bulged, his stories swelled with charm
his audience grew spellbound

All of you fell for us
We'd make you believe
you were in the valley of Anahuac
among oleander and banana trees
You'd swear you'd been with
the mythical warrior Popocatepetl
standing vigil for his lover Iztaccihuatl
Swear you'd seen Frida and Diego
on top of those snow capped volcanoes

Details

When Diego looks out at a field, he sees
the sprawling stories of Mexican Indians
political allegory, valiant struggles
for liberty, something universal
His people are all the same, brown with solid
bodies, round heads, their faces covered
with their hands or their hats. The only
difference among them is their hats
He sees the sunflowers and calla lilies, yes
But as for the women who pick them, he sees
only their thick black braids and their strong
brown backs as they kneel in the dirt, gathering
flowers in their arms. He sees what is on the outside

But when I look out at a field, I see inside
the sunflowers and calla lilies. I see the faces
of the women who pick them, the details
of what they wear, which one is skinny
which plump, how some can not keep their hair
combed, how the torn shirt and worn skirt
are the poverty and pride of Mexico

Inside the fruit and the flowers, inside the bodies
The small meanings that lie there

Witness

My mother opened our doors
to the wounded and the hungry
She fed them thick tortillas, the only food
we had during those tragic ten days in our city

My three sisters and I had a front row seat
to the violence outside our windows
on Allende Street, but at five years old
I was the one who cried for the Zapatista
with a bullet wound in his knee
and the man shot when he lingered
to buckle his sandals and the peasant
who limped by the river. I was the one
who learned the *corridos* I heard
sung in the *tianguis* of Coyoacán

My mother did not care for Zapata's peasants
or the Sonora generals. But she thought
our country might break in half
Every day the sound of hissing bullets

When I was seventeen
I changed my date of birth to coincide
with the Mexican Revolution
The dark wounds endured

Socialist Realism

It's like something out of Disney (that fascist)
Fantasia maybe, the way
American lark sparrows hover
in Central Park, tamed by greed
and human gesture to perform
for open hands filled with seed
No shame, these cartoon birds

But when Diego paints them, when
he sets them free in fields
and forests, they remember
who they are, tell him
their bird history, their bird
story. They remember then
their bird essence
and fly in exaltation
streaming

Mexicanidad 1930

Lucille Blanch in a velvet print dress
legs sprawled, wanton and submissive
she cuddles on Diego's spread-legged lap
tries to seduce the camera. His smile is salacious
as he hugs her firm against his body
Her cheek on his. Her one hand flung tight
around his neck, her other inching
towards his crotch

Arnold Blanch, tall thin blonde
wide white-toothed American grin, holds Frida
and she sits almost primly on his knees. She is sedate
and erect, hands crossed on her lap. Wears a long Mexican dress
and an Aztec choker around her neck. His arms try
to tighten round her waist, but his loosely laced fingers
do not confine her. She does not yield
her body to his

On the Border Between Mexico and the United States
Painted in 1932

We carouse with Manhattan's social elite
who eat and drink and glitter
against the backdrop of Diego's pageant
of sugar cane workers

Diego is so enchanted with Henry Ford's factories
and machines, so enamored of his own
grand symbolism, his idealized American
working class, he can't see
these modern temples are tombstones

But now he paints the head of Lenin
and Rockefeller throws him off the scaffold
They chip his mural from the wall
and smash it to white powder

Mexico feeds on the chimney stacks
of America. But in a cumulus Mexican sky
the sun spits fire, ignites a waning moon
The sky over Detroit belches
Ford's industrial smoke

The electrical cords of Gringolandia
are plugged into the lily-white roots
of my country. My nipples rise
hard under my pink gown

El Viejo

Trotsky's official biography barely mentioned me
They said he died in my country, yes
They wrote about Diego's admiration
for him. They said that the great man
lived and died in a house belonging
to the great painter, Diego Rivera, yes

They wrote about his proud revolutionary stride
his Russian blue scrutiny, gimlet-eyed
behind round tortoise shell glasses
his impeccable white hair, his even whiter
manicured whiskers

El Viejo always waited for his own death
so perhaps it was no surprise when it came, yes

They wrote that a follower of Stalin
entered Trotsky's study one humid day
at the end of August, an ice axe hidden
under his heavy overcoat. They said
he was struck a terrific blow to the skull
They described the piercing cry that would haunt
his assassin. Some suggested that Diego
organized the attack, but they did not say
I was arrested as a suspect
for the murder of Leon Trotsky

No, it was left for me to admit
how I missed the little goat
bored as I became by his clumsy fondle
under the table, his *billets doux* slipped
between the pages of a borrowed book

They have not written about the Leon I knew
The man released from graceless exile
They did not describe his delight in the rabbits
he kept hutched among the brilliant crimson flowers
of the hanging rat tail cactus or his pleasure
in the pink funnel blossoms of the succulents
he collected in his courtyard. They did not write
of the songbirds hanging in bamboo cages
from the jacaranda trees or how ripe the red
and yellow mango grew, wild, in his garden

Trotsky's Mock Trial

> Commission of Inquiry into the Charges Made Against
> Leon Trotsky in the Moscow Trials, headed by the
> American philosopher and educator, John Dewey, 1937

i.

What attracts them is the danger
and the drama. Diego directs it
as if painting a mural on the grand narrative
of history. A flick of his wrist and the windows
of the blue house are boarded up, eyes closed
to the outside world, lids filled in with red adobe brick

A theatrical gesture and the adjacent lot is bought
the neighbour evicted, the two properties connected
to prevent attack from the house next door
Barricades are erected around the gardens
and the courtyard. Bodyguards mingle with looming
six foot papier-mâché Judas figures that leer over the patio

Inside, Frida directs trusted servants to clear the stage
empties the living room, carries in a long oak table
set to face the forty chairs she groups for the audience
of invited guests. Eleven commissioners and John Dewey
sit at the rostrum, pose for photos as if in a surreal last supper
that will go on for seven days

Frida and Diego enter last, Frida decked out
in Trascan jewellery, Diego flaunting
a panama hat, peacock feather in the hatband
Their pet monkey Fulang perches on his shoulder
In they promenade as if to a command performance
after the journalists, photographers, officials
and even Trotsky himself. They sit at the front
Frida holds her sketchbook open in her lap

ii.

She paints the tribunal
The commissioners have the heads of dogs
Their teeth fanged. She colours them black
There are strings attached to their mouths
Dewey the puppet master, holds
the strings. Trotsky has a red pulsing heart
large gossamer wings glistening
with the golden faces of Marx, Lenin and Diego

After the trial she alters her sketch, shades
out the puppet strings, closes the mouths
of the dogs. Paints a hammer and sickle
on Dewey's forehead. She clips Trotsky's wings
Disconnected from his body, the wings
hover above them all

Natalia's Poem

Dear Leon, I am almost undone
by my Russian darkness. So unfitting
it must seem in the fantasia, this country
this overwhelm of green, relentless
blue, unforgiving sun. How is it
we have come to live in this sultry heat
and barrage of colour and sound?

What has become of us Leon?
How have I become this old woman?

Remember the barren cold of Alma Alta
the frigid pitch of the Black Sea? My sweet lion cub
do you remember at Constantinople we saw our son
Sergei for the last time? Lev and his brother both murdered
by Stalin. You and I on a pier day after day yearning
for a ship to come for us
We were so close then

I watch you grow animated and witty
when you are with Frida. Catch you fondle her knee
under the table, pass her love notes inside
the books you pretend to lend her. Speak to her
in English because you know I can't understand

Oh Leon, where is the comrade in her
—this seductive painter

Frida Reads the Tarot

The bougainvilleas are in full magenta bloom
White calla lilies sway under the weight
of erect yellow stamens. A row of poplar
hides the courtyard from the road
Maguay cactus and sapodilla trees line a path
to the garden where the albino peacock
and quetzals strut at will

Frida pours a glass of tequila
lights a black cheroot
Takes the deck of cards
and steps out into the courtyard

The clink of the glass
set down on the stone table
startles her spider monkeys. Guayabito
scrambles to the roof of the house
Fulang, her favourite, hears something
in the ring of glass on stone, jumps
to her shoulder and wraps his tail around her neck
The parrot ruffles its wings, tilts
a one-eyed disapproving glance
Frida settles on a high backed rattan chair

She lays the tarot, deals only the major arcana
her question about whether to end her affair
with Trotsky too important to leave
to the minor oracles. She flips the Magician first
The Magus can sell his ideas with one hand
and control a situation with the other. Yes
The next card tells what opposes the first
She turns the High Priestess, the unconscious
ruler of the dream world. Of course. Frida
drinks some tequila, draws on her cigar
Fulang swings down to her lap

One by one, the tarot continues
The Lovers, to explain the unconscious side
of her question. Temperance, for true will
The Devil in her past, the Moon in her future
The Sun for the face she shows the world
In the final position, Death
Card of transition

Fulang leaps to the ground
Frida leans back in her chair
A magenta petal from a jacaranda lands on the cards
She knows what she must do. She takes the petal
for its colour, leaves the courtyard for her studio
and begins to mix the paint

Self Portrait Dedicated to Leon Trotsky
Painted in 1937

The tincture of the paint is most important
Carmine ribbon and magenta jacaranda
braided through her dark hair. Crimson lips
rouged cheeks, wine dark blouse
The reds draw the eye
upward from the salmon of her skirt
and the yellow ochre of the rebozo shawl
The coquettish scarlet an antonym
to painting herself as a colonial woman
adorned in gold jewelry. She is standing
against a soft olive backdrop on a wooden floor
as if on a stage between white curtains
drawn open with heavy cord
A formal presentation to the world, to Trotsky
A gift of rejection

She composes it in the only way
he'll understand, stately and romantic
Nothing surreal except the way she appears
to float from between the curtains
as if she's just ended a performance
taken a bow and been handed
a small bouquet of flowers
A final forget-me-not

She holds her dedication to him
on a sheet of paper. Blood red
nail polish against the white

Assassination

I was bored with Trotsky. He was vain and I was tired of his
conceit. He was a coward. But it was a bad joke to say later we
only invited him to Mexico so Stalin could assassinate him. Diego
and I had nothing to do with it. Mercader hacked the old man's
skull with an ice axe all by himself

The police sacked Diego's house. Stole his drawings, paintings,
suits. My sister and I cried for two days in jail. Her little children
all alone in the empty house without food

Diego Recovers His Marxism

I watch Diego remove a large pistol from his coat. Place it on the table. Drape a handkerchief over the pistol and declare:

I, Diego Rivera General Secretary of the Mexican Communist Party accuse the painter Diego Rivera of collaborating with the petit-bourgeois government of Mexico by accepting a commission to paint the stairway of the National Palace. Therefore, the painter Diego Rivera should be expelled from the Communist Party by the General Secretary of the Communist Party, Diego Rivera

He stands up, removes the handkerchief. Smashes the pistol. It's made of clay

Marxism Will Give Health to the Sick
Painted in 1954

I want my paintings to shriek
and howl at the world. I want
the reasons for living and the reasons
for despair to intertwine and do battle
on the canvas. I have no breath
left for propaganda

I have nothing to say
No authority to say anything
But art must never be mute

The strong hands of the revolution
support me. I cast aside my crutches
and tear off my plaster corset
I have nothing left

For the first time
I am not crying

Henry Ford Hospital
   Painted in 1932

The hospital bed floats
over a dun coloured plain
Blood stained sheets against a deserted
Detroit horizon and pewter gray sky

This loss strips her naked
and tosses her into inarticulate space
Desolate stare. One amplified tear
on her cheek. Her belly swollen
with the missing child

She can barely grip her sorrow
Artery-red reins yoke her to the lost
fetus, her broken pelvis, salmon-red torso
and damaged spine. The snail slow abortion
The machine grip of pain and Diego's gift
the bruise coloured orchid

On her mantle she keeps
a fetus in a bottle of formaldehyde
Tells everyone
it's her own stillborn child

Roots
    Painted in 1943

Everything under the sun
is me. Stones, stars, birds
The universe of elaborate webs
Pain, struggle and death are me

I plant my body in the *pedregral*, the embrace
of stony earth, the entrails of volcanic rock
All the porous landscape, all the rough
grey crevices are me

I am life in a parched Mexican earth
I am toothy pods, snake like blossoms
Botanical dream. Red vesicles crack stone
Root me to earth

All the women who wail in the night
are me. All the dark ravines
all the caverns, all the graves
open at my feet

—Adapted from the diary of Frida Kahlo

A Parrot Screaming

She wore the Tehuana costume as a second skin
and even on her deathbed she dressed
as if for a fiesta. But no festive dress
could suppress the pain

Her palette, a rich needlework of colour
Long skirts of deep purples and red velvets
hand embroidered at the hem. Fringed
silk Spanish shawls and heavy pre-Columbian
necklaces. Ornate pendant earrings, bracelets
and rings that jangled as she walked
Her hair braided with vivid wool
ribbons, clips, bows and flowers

She dressed this way for Diego
and for her country but above all
she dressed to draw the eye away
from her fractured body
A parrot screaming in the jungle

Self Portrait as a Tehuana

Two self portraits; one painted in 1943 and the other in
1948

In the eyes he sees the difference
In the earlier painting she stares
from the canvas, a devouring spider
at the centre of a web. White tendrils spring
live wire from the *huipil* to the world
beyond the frame. Unrooted black tentacles
grope unruly for earth from the veins of green leaves
that adorn the bougainvillea and daisies in her hair

Diego smiles at his miniature likeness, a third eye
a portrait within a portrait painted on her brow
So like Frida to mimic the Catholic nuns
who hold the image of Christ
Does Frida dream she can capture him
or is she satisfied simply to trap
the thought of him on her forehead?

In the later canvas her face is composed
though the elaborate headdress seems
like a stage flat. The flowers are faded
and sere, the vegetation withered
in the background. She painted
three pearl teardrops on her cheeks

Can he see the turmoil, the rejection and rage
beneath her skin, the sadness in her eyes?

What She Knows From Painting Melons
Viva la Vida, painted in 1954

If it's a watermelon, the rind of the Golden Midget
turns yellow as it ripens, and a Sugar Baby
becomes a dark green before it loses its stripes
The ripe melon wears a powdery coat
and the leaf tendrils closest to the fruit dry and wither
She knows enough to pick a good one

She knows when to cleave a melon
to paint the ruby belly a sweet red wound
to fade its colour like its flavour as it edges
towards watery pink and white
with the loss of sugar towards the rind

If it's a muskmelon it might be a cantaloupe
a round, rough-skinned luscious Ambrosia
maybe a golden-yellow corrugated Casaba
Or it might be a smooth mute-skinned honeydew
a juicy Honeymoon, or Honey Brew
She paints the flesh of the fruit, each slice of orange
every sliver of summer-green or creamy white
perfect and the same. She's sure the taste
will never disappoint her

She knows that a melon will tell you
when it's ready to reveal its secrets
That once you split it open
what you know from painting a melon
is what you can count on. When she paints
its flesh, she understands about soil
about seed, about earth
about everything

The Canvas

A desert shiver when she feels
it coming. The vast sea of volcanic rock
the fault, the fissures dammed with the smooth spin
of jade, blood red tears of the sun. The bloom
of the canvas, the jungles, forests, sudden flowers

The protective wall of leaves. One single
leaf always painted in reverse, *doblar la boja*
The monkeys that cling to her, surrogate
children, their paws wrapped
around her neck, their fingers ginger
in her braided hair

She paints the stare of a woman railing
unable to free herself from the fragments
of alliteration, sound and sense
sound and sense

The Frame
    Painted in 1938

This is the painting they buy
to put in the Louvre in Paris
this stinking city of philistines
this city of self-serving fakes
They put my jeweled hand on the cover
of Vogue, they design a 'robe Mme Rivera'
in my honour. To hell with Breton
and this lousy place. These French
'intellectual' artists disgust me

I'd rather sit on the floor in the market of Toluca
and sell tortillas than have anything to do
with those "artistic" bitches of Paris

Miró hugs me. Kandinsky kisses me
Picasso gives me a gift of earrings, beautiful
tortoise shell hands with gold cuffs. But to Breton
and the others I am a Mexican trophy
Only a woman could embody their exotic idea
of Mexico. Patronizing bastards

I am not crafting a decorative object
Look closely. The periphery becomes
more intricate, the boundary more vivid
than the woman in the centre
who is no longer fully there

This is what a woman
looks like when she is vanishing

mad

this is
the painting
you've been
wondering about
the one
you'll never
ask me
about

the one
that makes you
think
the one
where you
will never be
sure

how much
is a lie
how much
conjecture and
how much
depends upon
how much
honesty
means to me

My Body Is Plunged In Oranges

A Union of Lions

There are dark places in all of us Diego
You say
yours may be bottomless
You say
you have need of yours
You say
that a part of you feeds
on that darkness
and you are lost in it

That point where one has
no control

I meet you there

I say
your darkness
is betrayal

Beauty has the shape
of your neck Frida
the turn of your lip
the toss of your hair
And in one of those moments
of real passion, I almost
bend down to whisper I love you

But we are jealous lovers
And the beast I am
never unwillingly
is yours
and has always been
the beast
you were looking for

Gnostic Serenade

What would I have become
if I hadn't watched you paint
those murals in the Preparatoria
Searing notes of music. A string
wound tightly round my heart

Now you walk away
from the repeating melody
line. For me it is still
everything. You risk
its loss forever

Ah, but we have been intense lovers
Each straining for supremacy
Drawn to each other
in mutual resistance
and desire

You are the Mirror of the Night

violent lightning
damp earth
Your green sword eyes slice my flesh
Your words are chained in my cells
as words we could not say
except with the lips of sleep

Your touch permeates the tips of my fingers
You are the thick of oak, the memory of walnut
the green breath of ash. The blood of the pomegranate
is the juice of your lips

You are the universe. Your absence is the tremble
in the pulse of light. I am with you a minute
and I am with you forever and my blood
is the miracle that travels in the veins
of the air from my heart to yours

Nothing compares to your hands on my body
You penetrate the sex of the whole earth
Your heat embraces me, covers my body
with fresh tender leaves

Only a mountain knows the inside of another mountain
My life in your hands, in your mouth
My body surrounded by you, plunged in oranges

— adapted from the journals of Frida Kahlo

Roads Are Not Travelled in Vain

Everything changes
Everything moves
Everything. Everything flies away
and vanishes

Change and struggle terrify
We anticipate the death we die
at every second. To be alive is to feel
the anguish of waiting for the next minute
not knowing

The joys and sorrows of this society
rotten with lies, are not mine
If I am hurt by others, even Diego
if I feel locked in without time
or magic, within great anguish
in my very heartbeat
it is my own madness

Nobody will ever understand
how much I love Diego
how I can let nothing hurt
him or rob him of energy
to paint, love, be by himself
or with someone else
to live like a seed
the earth treasures

Diego was never mine
and never will be

I am a green point in a sea of red

I want to paint him

but the colours don't exist
And in my confusion
the concrete form
of my great love
doesn't exist

This life, this giver of worlds, morning
dawns, red friends, great blue spaces
noisy birds, nests of doves, fingers
in my hair, madness
of the wind in my heart

The simplicity of the song of injustice
is a storm in the blood that enters by mouth

—adapted from the diary of Frida Kahlo

The Two Fridas
Painted in 1939

I live as two Fridas
I am European. I am Tehuana
I love men. I love women
Two Fridas, and both our hearts
exposed and both connected
by a fragile artery

The blood of one Frida stems
from you Diego and feeds the other
and my blood is the miracle that flows
from my heart to yours
This doubling of myself only deepens
the chill of loneliness

I try to clamp the blood flow
between us, but it drips Diego
It pools and puddles between my legs
It stains the folds of the hem
on my European dress like embroidered red flowers
But Mexican Frida only wears the colours
of madness and mystery

Two Fridas Diego
Each depends on the other
Neither can let the other go

Paris Dreaming 1939

You are in the palm-lined streets
of Coyacoán, dreaming of the volcanos
that rise above the city, of pyramids carved
out of calla lilies and a great barrel-cactus
on which the eagle perches
clutching a serpent in its claws

I am dreaming in Paris
And in my dream walls are crumbling
and I must move us out of danger
And still inside my dream, I awake
with a start and know we have left
our monkey Fulang locked in the basement
of the ruins of the Louvre, and it's been a week
and he must be starving, no, he must be dead
from hunger. And in my dream
I am terrified to go and open the basement door
and face what I have done

While you are still in Mexico, dreaming
of your three story murals in the Palacio Nacional
dreaming of the feathered serpent Quetzalcoatl
lord of the wind and the air
I dream again of hunger, of an orange cat
we keep in the cellar of Casa Azul
who chases mice beneath my easel. You plead
with me to bring the cat upstairs, but I don't know
what to feed a cat, can't she live
on the mice she catches?
and in my dream I know she will starve

In your dreams
Every morsel is delicious
And the markets are overflowing with fruit

In my dream I lean forward and take
a sharp bite out of your lip
Is it hunger or hostility I hallucinate
in the country of my dreams, where
you and I stand in a large clearing
There is a gun in my hand
I pull the trigger, a warning
shot? before you disappear for good

When I come home from Paris
you dream you raise baby sparrows
set them free, shoo them out our garden door
and away they all fly, up
over the prickly cactus that guards
the door to your studio

I too dream of baby sparrows, but mine
nest in the rubble of our cellar
their scrawny necks stretched out
their beaks wide open and straining for food
and I am helpless to feed them. When I reach
for them, they are balls of dust, and my touch
scatters them to motes that float in the air

Infidelity

because women adored him
because so many wanted to be
with a man who doted on them
who courted them, was attentive
appreciative. Because so many
were enamored of his fame
or wanted to play beauty to his beast

because he was always hungry
for pleasure, was tender
and deeply sensuous and because
he had the artist's appetite
for what he could see and touch

I want to say that he took pleasure
with many women but that he desired
me the most. I want to say
that I was the only one
he loved

Silent Lover

She found a lover
who had no need to tell
and no need to ask
She never knew his name

She loved best his silence
how he could believe
there was no need
to know. He saved her
in his vacant room void
of light but for the dirty
yellow glow of a veladora

There were no questions
In all their time together
they spoke no more
than a few dozen words

How could anyone lose
desire for a lover
with an inner life?

She only wanted her emptiness
to be filled by his

Portrait of an Icon

I slipped out of my blouse
shivered naked to the waist
stared straight into the camera's
milky black eye, its focus
a lover's stroke, a shudder
across my bare skin and slowly

I removed each
tortoise shell comb
from my hair, let the long
strands fall free, ripple loose
to my shoulders, caress my back
brush lightly across my nipples
and his camera aroused

me. And I wound my fingers
a tease of liturgy
through each heavy plait
of dark hair, braided it
with silk ribbons and flowers
pulled and twisted it tightly
dug the combs into my scalp
sweet pain, raised my arms
to sweep the hair upwards
so that my breasts swelled

for his camera. And he took me
with his camera and I gave myself
to his camera and I said
here I am do not forget me

Love Embrace of the Universe, the Earth (Mexico), Diego, Me and
Señor Xolotl
     Painted in 1949

On that day, I opened the door
to what I thought was just another
famous actress come to model for him
But I opened the door to you Maria
and was caught, held breathless
by your bravado and your beauty. Mesmerized
by possibility, by your sullen mouth
and the delicious flesh of your lip

I could see that you knew your way around
our house. I saw how your fingers
were familiar with each crease
in the sheets of our bed

You said Diego wanted to marry you
and you couldn't live
without him. For the first time
I thought how possible it might be
to give him up

I Will Always Write to You With My Eyes

I am sorry for not writing to you
before. I have not forgotten
you or the color of your skin
or your eyes. The wind of Mexico
still reminds me of your hair
The *huipil* with purple ribbons
is you. I am the old plazas of your Paris
I can't escape the memory of those days
with you and I can't return to that time
The nights are long and difficult
Keep me in your heart

The water. The boat and the pier
and the departure. Later came
long days without you

But you know that everything I touch
is Diego. The caress of cloth, color
nerves, pencils, paper, dust and the sun
All that lives in the minutes of no-clocks
and no calendar is him

You felt this. You let the boat
carry me from Le Havre
You never said good bye

       —adapted from a letter written by Frida Kahlo to an
       unknown lover in Paris

Comet

I trail you like a lesser moon
tonight, a night suddenly sprinkled
in unease, stars spilled pell-mell
in sharp relief against the deep dark sky

Tonight I keep a deliberate
pace behind you, not sure
if I should walk in step beside you
or turn out of your orbit, spin
all alone into the universe

I want to lie down
in the middle of the road
and fall up into the night sky
I want to hear just one deep
shuddering truth in my ear

Tonight Orion grabs your attention
not me. But that bright star
you point to when you turn
and wait for me to catch up
is really a comet, a one-shot visitor
that won't return in a million years

Magnolias
　　　Painted in 1945

Naturaleza muerta we say in Mexico
But you and I Diego, we say *naturaleza viva*

Your calla lily a symbol of sorrow
and death for the workers who pick them
You paint their solitary funnels unfurling
in a mass of showy spathes

In the *aquilegia* you see the talons of an eagle
I turn the flower upside down to see
the columbine, the doves perched
around a water fountain, drinking

My still life bursts and squirts and weeps
I slice it open, expose its flesh
its suffering submerged deep
inside its vegetal being

I paint magnolias, *flors de corazón*
porcelain white, their cool petals closed
I do not let you inside
my heart-shaped leaves

Look closely Diego to see
the prickly cactus stem
at the centre of my bouquet
One of its stamens has been snapped
Know that once picked, a cactus flower
cannot be kept alive

Yours Was A Red Kiss

Who I am when I am
with you I want to be
again

Now my mouth only imagines
itself on yours and my heart
is a burgled swallow's nest

And I am wrapped inside the memory
of watching Christina comb her long wet hair
down her breast and you
sitting on a morning kitchen stool
Your half smile, your whole smile
Your mouth

Me watching your eyes
as you hold her, trail your finger
down her cheek, touch her lip
Your mouth
Your mouth

And I flinched
when you smiled at me
then turned away as if you struggled
between a moan and a sigh

I only wanted to be
a match to your heart
depth to your light
Instead I am a cold wind
crawling up your back

Triptych

How you could let me
find you like that?
Do you resent me?
Despise me?

I never wanted you
to pose for him
But you did it anyway
All the time
In the nude

I am the talented sister, the artist
I have the fame
But you are the pretty one
The one he wants
to paint. His favourite
He told me that

Look my sister, how he paints you
elegant, feminine and proud
how he paints me homely
plain and insignificant. How
we hang together for all to see
in the Palace Nacional

In spite of everything
I love you

Morning After

Frida stares out an open door
to the sun-daze of her garden
All flurry in the trees strangely absent
All bird song broken

A spider monkey freezes half way up
a banana tree. High in the grass green
needles of a weeping pine, she sees
the yellow gaze of a falcon
the gleam as it eyes a *tangara escarlata*
on the *cempasúchil*, the almost
imperceptible flinch before it launches
all talon, sharp beak, spreading wings

She watches the falcon snatch the tanager
from the flower of the dead, watches
the shock of the small bird caught
in that one moment of pure clarity

The falcon plucks its prey alive, feather by feather
Blood spatters on the patio stones
He stares her straight in the eye
as he tears the fresh meat from the small bones

Nausea

I completed three paintings
over three nights
while the tension flowed
over the white table top
cold and stained between us

you were talking
but I was empty and aching
and I'm sorry
but I just couldn't sit there any longer
with you when your very existence
in my life forces me to this
I don't have the strength to try
and understand why
you did this to me
and I want you to know
that it took supreme
physical and mental effort
to say anything at all
however trivial
and walk away

Memory
Painted in 1937

My heart
a throb on bare ground
Blood defying gravity

My past and my present
bound together by the thinnest
crimson. Dis-armed, forsaken
on the border between water and earth

A gaping hole empties me
leaves me a human fulcrum
Two tiny cupids seesaw a delicate balance

Las Lagrimas

Mi ninita chiquitita, he writes
It would be best for both of us
if you will consent to divorce

And each syllable of his letter
echos a deep rumble
Dusk turns a ghostly silver, turns
the Snowy Egrets preternaturally white
the calla lilies uncanny, pure
the smooth grey bark of the strangler fig
incandescent. Its roots melt
into one another, into the rocks of her garden

The sky thickens as flock after flock
of black birds flap overhead
and the air chokes

Lightning releases the sky

And then it comes
it comes like rain

After the Divorce

A shift in the weather
Today you are gone
and I am here at the water's edge, ready
to swim out into the sea, a storm
rolling in, the dark horizon inciting
the waves. They call. I answer

There is a heat in me Diego
A wave crazed gulf
My storm. The ocean's storm

The return to shore
So easy to be taken
So hard the coming back
The way the waves tumble you
pitch you helpless
against them, crash you
into the boulders, push you, pull you
Hold you

Self Portrait With Cropped Hair
Painted in 1940

What happens when your bones grow
but your skin won't stretch
to fit over them?

What happens when you can't tell day from night?

Why am I so cold?
So cold my body cannot move

Cannot move from this yellow chair
from this blood-yellow room
this gathering acid sky

In my right hand, scissors
A whet-sharp blade on my lap
A lock of my own hair hangs
like a dead animal
between my legs

I strip off my Tehuana masquerade
Wear Diego's baggy suit
Sit, legs apart, like a man
in this barren room

My hair, my hair

Cut it. Cut it all off

See my desire still
writhe, still twist and coil
in a frenzied life of its own

Day of the Dead

This night, all hallow's eve
when the veil between
our worlds is most gossamer
and *la dia de los muertos*
is upon us, I mask myself
with the skull of the lady
of the dead, and call for you

When *la dia de Todos Santos*
swells the throat of night sky
I light a single taper
burn *copal*, lay the tarot
on fresh linen. I decorate
the altar with marigolds
cockscomb and chrysanthemum

I bake bones of meringue
marzipan skeletons, prepare
sugar skulls with your name
on their foreheads. I dance
for you, wear the crimson wings
of a bird of madder orange
and scatter vermilion feathers
along a path to guide you back to me
I wait for you
and the souls of the dead
to come home

Frida Dreams Diego

I dream of you Diego
I dream I am at a long table
and a woman comes to me
and places a book down before me
says *Diego told me to give this to you*
it's a book about how to paint endings
And I ask *How do you know Diego?*
But there you are beside me
to tell me you can show me
how to paint an ending
And you ask me to come with you
and I do and we stand in front of a locked door
You tell me how the woman behind the door
has the answer and you have the key
But you search your pockets and there is no key

And we're walking over land that stretches so far
I have no idea where it will end
And we're walking faster and faster
I carry a dark green flimsy bamboo cane
And we touch. Your right side touches
my left and your hand is on me, guiding me
My cane breaks. I'm startled and look around

You are gone
To my left, two ballet dancers
a man and a woman. She's beautiful, but thin
like cardboard, holds her body stiff
He's able to lift her with just two fingers
And I think—oh Diego must see this
I look behind me and I see you Diego
You're wearing red and you wave to me
but you're far away
I turn back to the dancers, but they're gone

And then you're there beside me and your face
is harsh and old in the light
and you're agitated and you say
I am hungry, I am so hungry
And we're at a *chiringuito*
There's a cook and a woman to take your order
We sit there on stools in the middle of nowhere
and you tell her what you want to eat
but she doesn't understand
and I explain to her everything you want
and she smiles at me

You and I on the lawn, heat close
facing each other and I say
I understand. I know how to paint the ending
We have to blur the edges. You say
You think too much. Stop thinking
and I say *You disconnect your words from*
from what you do and I lean over
to place my fingers on your lips
to place my hand upon your mouth

The Divine Gift

Finally I understand, Diego
We thought we could have it
both ways. Swallow the power
in a covenant at the crossroads
and walk away

But the vow, once taken,
can never be denied
or taken back. It's the pact
that squeezes the soul dry
as your dreams unfold
and your wishes come true

Each betrayal is a solitary journey
that begins with good-bye. And those
we leave behind suffer. Now I
who stay behind, I am trapped
within my own imagining
blinded inside my own betrayals

I want to explain this to you
before we part ways forever

I never expected this to happen
I never expected
to become addicted to you

Remarriage 1940

In the photo from their first marriage
the groom, six feet tall, stands
in grizzly bulk beside his bride
No vest. His three hundred pounds
protrude over his belt and out his open grey suit jacket
His smile is pleased. He is a bear
who has just scooped a fish from the river
His right arm is heavy around her. In his left hand
he holds a cowboy hat, that if placed on his bride's head
would fall to her shoulders

The bride sits beside the groom
shoulder tiny in his cupped paw. She
does not wear traditional white, but
skirt and blouse, a shawl borrowed
from the maid. She sits with her legs crossed
stares with trademark intensity
at the camera. Her right hand dangles
a cigarette. It's the bride who leads us
to think we can predict what lies ahead

In the photo from their second marriage
the black and white image is sharp and clear
The bride and groom share equal space
They are both seated. His face is serious
over his pen, his bulk takes up less room
Her ringed hand rests on his shoulder
Her Tihuana skirt and blouse
are elaborately embroidered cotton
a pre-Columbian bead necklace
heavy around her throat

Thirty-one years have passed
She is still beautiful, still intense
She looks down at the papers
to be signed, not at the camera
We believe we can see
their whole story—the sorrow that came before
the suffering that came after

I Am A Storm Beaten Window

The Shadow of Everything Existing

She has an instinct
for the shadow's descent
Night's breath exhaled
as a vapour silhouette
on the cold stone walls
along the avenues

She stalks the dark
like a sculptor who molds deep
blue sound, but is held
motionless before a symphony
that can not bear
movement

She turns to what's forgotten
a dark that will not be
taken, that will not retreat
a dark not conquered
by light

In that dark
Frida stands
a figure of sound
stark and white
and calling

Amputation

Awake in an indigo blue dream   so much time lying here   is she
home   is this her hospital room   is this the sky all iris bleed to
azure pink   is that Diego in the mask of a jaguar perched on her
window sill   is that Christina   blister amber eyes dissipating
smoke   a grinning skull

Awake in a glaucous kaleidoscope fever   is this broken glass
she lies on or is it bone that will not fuse to her spine   stitches
that pull and ache   wounds that won't close   is this stench the
deep humus musk decay of her garden or the stink of her own rot
abscess under the damp plaster corset prison   and the noise   is
she lying in a jungle of macaws   and is this a parrot screaming or
her own voice that scores the edge of beryl consciousness

Awake   they appear as if through the wrong end of a telescope
four bruise blue necrotic toes   this is her right foot bulging red
bronze   her putrid reek   these are her black stumps fallen to the
sheets

This is her leg they will take below the knee

Disintegration

this pain and my body
crawls back inside itself
this pain and i am a live body
dissected, fragmented, an assembly
of malfunctioning parts
this pain gouges everything
i am made of
everything i am

as if nails pierce my flesh
a hammer crushes my bones
your arrow impales my heart

and my body is cut open
is transparent, turned inside out

this pain and my face
shows you nothing
only a single tear

Fugue

hair long and loose she sits
in verdant vegetal ontology

a straight-backed chair, her garden
a leafy jungle. the flora, their stomata

the small pores in the silky underside
of their leaves and stems, beckon

a row of single eyes bound
by two half moon guards

eyelids protecting a slow wink
they purse like the gape-mouths of fish

pulse and suck in a chloroplast kiss
lure her into each watery cell

to breathe with them, their inhale
and exhale the life ascending tendrils and stalk

as intrinsic as mitosis
an inducement to suicide

We Are Stars Frida

Light is born
in the death of a star
and we are stars Frida
We are hot
incandescent spheres
spinning disks of dust
floating in deep sky
We burn Frida
We radiate heat

We live to implode
under the pull
of our own gravity
Hurl ourselves
into a dark infinity
Free fall willingly

We will die
as we are born you and I
Explode in burning light
Only to be born again

I Am A Storm-Beaten Window

i

Sweet relief
you bring to me sympathy
for all things
(sail, sail away)

Your kiss slips
heaven's breath
through my veins
(come, come away)

Slow now, sweet shiver
i wait for you
in half light
(slide, slide away)

See me now
the way i am
Thin thief of life
Hear me breathe
through the eye of a needle
and so to fade
(fade away)

ii.

relief is sapphire
streaming shades of blue
a hawk tracing infinity
fading into heaven

my eyes glitter marble
glow damask
into the dark

until somewhere
an oboe moans
release

and i am on my way down the path
i can't stop for the blue or the black
and i know i never will

i drink from my palm
clean and clear
let the air serve my bones

and there are drifts
where my memory has been

iii.

tonight the light rises
howling green, drains
to deadly white

it's so cold

i flex my fingers
and all my skin comes
rushing
rushing to me

(keep your hand moving)
swerve
(keep you mind moving)
swerve
don't get caught, swerve

it's so cold

the timbre of the light
shatters in tin
fractures

flesh restrained until the hit
and echoes of consciousness
plunge backward, crumble
into tangerine vibration

my head in slow motion
through thick air streams
images of itself into infinity
on through the dark and fades
to a red dust quiver

when i look down i am
telescoping into a linoleum flower
painted on my bedroom floor

it's so cold

iv.

i prowl back alleys
like distorted tilting mirrors
Lurk in their reflection
Recoil from their memory
Like an avalanche they pass quickly

i need more
You are guilty of conspiring
to construct an altar
but one of your hearts is not pure

Bastardos
More

v.

Tonight
i feel as if i've been waiting
for something to happen
and now, it has

i don't know
if you've ever been tempted
by the devil or the Lord
i don't know if you've ever
seen a tin angel
But i had it all wrong
i thought
it was a love song

i let you follow me down
Let you pull the needle
Let you see my skin turn yellow
Sure there were light fractures
Blessed relief
We climbed Iztaccihuatl to pray for me
But where were we really?
You professed to know the tin angel
Ah, but you thought it was gold

i thought i knew your heart
But those furious blue veins
under your shell smile
only carry your heart away

Watch over me carefully
even with the eyes you use
on everything
i reflect
but i do not look back

vi.

i drop down
through shadow
stainless steel vibration
splitting consciousness
razor sharp
as each piece falls away
crumbless   clean

i disconnect
as if i'd moved out of casa azul
given up carpets and candles
forgotten the blues and greens
it no longer matters
as long as i get
connection

and if i listen very closely
i can hear what they're saying

though i think it's funny
how some people talk
and say nothing and
some people never have to open
their mouths and say everything

but it's okay
i always make it
sun to sun   circle back again
blues and greens streaming

and in the last few precious moments
before the shadow falls
i'm always forgiven

vii.

Cathedral bells toll through the rain
and i'm sitting among flakes of water
surrendering piece by crooked piece to you
to have them placed before i am sucked up
into the sky, to the arms of the sun at last
and lose consciousness

i have never needed anyone as desperately
as i needed you and your words
a half hour before you spoke them
i wonder if you will ever need mine as badly

Even in the present i hold you in memory
Some pre-Columbian art we once held as sacred

In the weary hours of the early morning
i begin to focus again
and i wish you were beside me
Everything blurs and rearranges
It's raining and your face dissipates and dissolves
i can still hear you sing through the thunder

Blue For Distance

Blue, the scatter of light
lost in air, the depth of the ocean
the deep dream melancholy
blue of the horizon
where it dissolves into sky
at the edge of the world

Blue for distance
for solitude. The desire
for there seen from here
For where she could never go

Sweet shiver of blue
The relief it brings her
How it slips like silk

The Altruism Of A Last Syringe

How everything depends
on silence. How the body
no longer storms, no longer
thrashes against the mystery

How something inside her
opens to the mountains
and volcanoes, to the roots
and trees, to a botanical dream
gone dark

How like a lover
rising from her own body
it takes her last breath
into the night

How in the end
everything turns away

The Blue House
Coyoacán, July 13, 1954

Her mother told her about the rain
the opaque curtain of rain, relentless
outside the room where she was born
downstairs in this very house

And all her life she loved the rain
It watered her garden, bathed
the paving stones in the courtyard
washed her blue walls clean
She always slept in the room
she was born in, the one beside
her studio, and now she gazed through
the open doorway, losing herself once more
inside the rain, letting it blur the edges
of her pain, letting it lose her inside its torrent

She gave the house the name *Casa Azul*
It embraced her solitude, witnessed
her life. It held the rooms of her broken body
and the beds of her illness. On its walls
hung the mirrors of her revelation. Inside it
she lived her art. And inside it, she always said
she was dying

The house was as she always kept it
Outside a deep unyielding blue
Inside, the floors red for the colour of blood
the walls yellow for madness and for sun and joy
the wainscoting blue for distance, but for tenderness too
The windows and doors she left open
to the rain and to the birds
and to the people who always came

It rained for days after she died
Inside the blue house, they placed
her ashes and her death mask wrapped
in a rebozo shawl on the centre of her bed

Glossary

Aquilegia columbine

Cachuchas a political group of students named for the caps they wore at the National Preparatory School

Casa Azul the Blue House

Cempasúchil Flower of the Dead

Chiringuito a small bar that sells food and beverage

Copal a type of resin produced by plants and trees ceremonially burned as incense

Corrido a popular narrative song, a ballad

Cursi corny and vulgar

Doblar la boja turning a leaf—refers to Kahlo's habit painting one leaf in reverse

Flor de Corazon heart of the flower

Huipal traditional embroidered dress worn by Mexican Indian women

La Dia de los Meurto Day of the Dead

La Dia de Todos Santos All Saints Day

Mesitaje refers to the popular reform movement of José Vasconcelos

Naturaleza muerte still life

Naturaleza viva   still life

Ninita chiuitita   term of endearment

Novio   fiancé

Pedregal   stony earth, volcanic rock

Pulqué   an alcoholic beverage made from the fermented juice of the maguey

Tangara escarlata   scarlet taninger

Tianguis   open public market